JAMES
BOND'S
WORLD OF
VALUES

LYCURGUS M. STARKEY, JR.

ABINGDON PRESS   NASHVILLE - NEW YORK

JAMES BOND'S WORLD OF VALUES

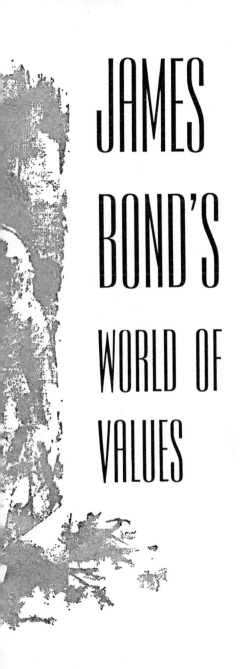

JAMES BOND'S WORLD OF VALUES

Copyright © 1966 by Abingdon Press

Library of Congress Catalog Card Number: 67-11015

Scripture quotations unless otherwise noted are from
the Revised Standard Version of the Bible, copy-
righted 1946 and 1952 by the Division of Christian
Education, National Council of Churches, and are
used by permission.

The first four chapters of this book were originally pre-
sented on "Frontiers of Faith," sponsored by the Broad-
casting and Film Commission of the National Council
of Churches, and are used by arrangement with the
National Council; "The Manly Art of Seduction" is
used by permission of *Good Housekeeping Magazine.*

SET UP, PRINTED, AND BOUND BY THE
PARTHENON PRESS, AT NASHVILLE,
TENNESSEE, UNITED STATES OF AMERICA

TO COLLEGE AVENUE
METHODIST CHURCH

CONTENTS

A
PREVIEW......... 9

1 THE MANLY
ART OF
SEDUCTION ...17

2 THE
VIOLENT
ONES 35

3 SNOBBERY
MADE
SIMPLE.......51

4 THE
PLEASURE
SEEKERS......64

5 FOR
LOVE OF
COUNTRY 79

Thirteen novels and four movies have poured from the pen of Ian Fleming and have mushroomed into a "hula-hoop" fad of major proportions. James Bond, the secret-agent hero of the series, has become an international hero. With his code name 007, Bond has moved into the retail fields of men's toiletries and pajamas. *Variety* claimed there would be an 007 toy under nine out of ten Christmas trees. The novels have been translated into ten languages and have sold in the neighborhood of eighteen million copies. *Playboy* magazine has given its imprimatur to the series by publishing serially the last of Fleming's novels, *The Man with*

A PREVIEW

9

the Golden Gun. The Bond fad or cult has created a new demand for secret-agent-spy thrillers on television, with more than one network scrambling to suppy a "Bond" type series.

What are we to make of this? Why is James Bond so popular? Are we to put it all down as a wonderful way to escape, as my bookseller put it; a delightful time replacement, as Sean Connery described it? Is Ian Fleming trying to spoof us with an overdrawn caricature of our own exaggerated sex, sadism, and snobbery? Some have seen it as spoof. James Bond is too blown up to believe, but exciting, action-packed narrative to read. Or is James Bond a hero type for modern man—"immorality serving the public good, a combination that proved irresistible to an age dedicated to affluence and to being with it." [1] I suspect there are many who have swallowed Bond and his set of values as a quite credible master to imitate, a public image whose whoring and wheeling and dealing give some of us a little more confidence in our

[1] *Time*, August 24, 1964, p. 37.

own indiscretions. Agent 007 is popular because he reflects a world of values subscribed to and aspired to by many in our affluent, rootless culture today.

It is useless to try and censor the books and the movies. They have inundated the public sphere to flood stage. Besides, they are too exciting and entertaining to avoid. But some ethical appraisal from a Christian point of view is needed to sort out the value system so strongly sustained throughout the Bond cycle.

There are five major areas in which James Bond's world of values challenges the Christian faith and ethic. They are the areas of sex, sadism, status, leisure time, and a narrow nationalism. In each of these areas I will isolate the Bond reflection of a current value. Then I hope to show the distortion of life which such a value holds before modern man.

The first chapter is entitled "The Manly Art of Seduction." The current *Playboy*-Bond assumption that every female is just waiting and wanting to be seduced is an unreal male myth of rubbish proportions. What about the current plea for premarital sexual experimentation in the name of commonsense realism? Some clergy are making headlines by justifying this in the name of love, just as some want to bury God.

The Christian faith can show such man-handling of the female and even affection without responsibility to be self-destructive. The sacredness of persons and the loyalty that belongs to true love point to the logic of the marriage bond for sexual relations.

Chapter two is entitled "The Violent Ones." Running through the Bond saga is the celebration of sadism and the constant appeal to violence as the solution of every conflict between so-called good and obvious evil. There seem to be those on every hand—newspaper editors, teen-age hooligans, legionnaires, and repressed minorities who are itching to fight on the slightest provocation. The Christian ethic does provide alternatives to violence for the sake of honor or pleasure, and more than a rule, it does provide a motivation and capacity to love and be loved.

In chapter three we will take a look at

"Snobbery Made Simple." The appeal to status, the cultivation of snobbery in our society, is reflected in Bond's lowbrow acquirement of aristocratic tastes. His catalogue of brand names for his consumption of alcohol, racing cars, and gourmet meals suggests the motivational research of a Madison Avenue advertising firm. Why this anxious worrying and scurrying to move up the social ladder, to be what we are not in superficial terms? Does it not suggest the basic hunger of the human heart for a perfection that eludes us, a transcendence that haunts us? The snob symbols are finally deceptive. The status-seeking wisdom of this passing age is folly with God who exalts the humble and grants his kingdom to the meek. But to prove the simplicity of it—this is the challenge.

"The Pleasure Seekers" are our concern in chapter four. We are in the midst of a fun explosion, a leisure time revolution. How will modern man use his new free time to do as he pleases? Bond advocates gambling, guzzling, sports car gunning, and gourmandising—in short, the conspicuous consumption of one's

13

leisure time and resources for the titillation of one's own nerve ends. Do we not see here the overanxious conscience worried about saving the self? The Christian faith enables us to joyfully celebrate life, accept ourselves and others in the reality of God's acceptance.

Our fifth and final chapter assesses the ultimate norm for Bond's business pursuits, "For Love of Country." Demagogues and scoundrels have always waved the flag and insinuated treason in others to boost their own standing in the community. Some who call themselves patriots want to stifle all criticism of the nation and resort to simple, inward-looking solutions for world problems. They guard the status quo, prevent healthy renewal, and contribute to a national *rigor mortis*. Unknowingly they idolize the state and phase God out. But only a nation and a world under the God and Father of our Lord Jesus Christ can fulfill their destiny.

One final note for the new faddists in theology and ethics. Just remember, in all your concern for that immediate situation or context, don't make the mistake of stepping out of

14

the human race, as Paul Tillich warned. In your concern for experience (still a good word in my vocabulary) be sure you bite off a two-thousand-year chunk of it. "To the Word and the Testimony," as John Wesley put it, and *then* to the immediate "situation." There may still be a place for community consensus, rules of thumb subject to review, and moral stands for the church. There's certainly no time for red-blooded American boy and girl types to figure out what *agape, eros,* and *philia* would have them do next while necking in the back seat of a car. Dr. Graham B. Blaine, Jr., chief of psychiatry at Harvard University Health Services, told a recent meeting of the Academy of Religion and Mental Health that young people need and secretly want "clearly defined guidelines." But what they often get—from churches as well as parents—is a lot of vague talk about morality being dependent upon circumstances. Theologians who strive for modernity, he said, may believe that they are appealing to young people when they assure them the only absolute requirement of Christian morality

15

is to love God. But in fact, they are "failing to provide the firm guidance that young people need and inwardly seek." Thank God for some moral positions. Let's try to nail some down for our day and age.

I must not fail to acknowledge the critical appraisal and support from Miss Doris Ann, N.B.C. Producer, and Marvin Einhorn, N.B.C. Director; Robert Currie, National Council of Churches Producer, and Jim Kaye, Director for the N.C.C., in the original presentation of four of these chapters as lectures on the "Frontiers of Faith" series. I am especially indebted to Mrs. Donald Marshall and Mrs. Lynden Mitchell, secretaries of College Avenue Church, who typed and teased the chapters into better shape.

The manly art of seduction—that suits James Bond to a tee. Only twice in thirteen novels does he fail to seduce the girl he fancies. "With most women his manner was a mixture of taciturnity and passion. The lengthy approaches to a seduction bored him almost as much as the subsequent mess of disentanglement."[1] Mr. Bond's primary concern is the passion of an animal function. But what's manly about corrupting or debauching the ladies—and what real man would have to hit and run? It would seem that Agent 007 can't face the music of responsible, adult male-female relationships.

Whether Bond be spoof

1 THE MANLY ART OF SEDUCTION

[1] *Casino Royale*, p. 120.

or truth, let us say that Fleming's popular novels point to a world of sexual values entertained by many. The traveling salesman jokes and James Bond are in the same category—we may enjoy the story but the moral decay implied is not so funny. And where is the moral decay, you say? Well, examine the sexual assumptions in the Bond books, in the Kinsey report, in some of Billy Wilder's movies, in *Playboy's* play for profit.

The Kinsey reports of a few years back pointed to widespread sexual promiscuity in America. Kinsey reported 67 percent [2] of college men and 60 percent [3] of college women to have experienced premarital intercourse. Lower the educational level, and the percentage increased for the men according to his research. Fifty percent [4] of all women are not virgin at mar-

[2] Kinsey, Pomeroy, and Martin, *Sexual Behavior in the Human Male* (Philadelphia: W. B. Saunders Co., 1948), p. 552.

[3] Kinsey, Pomeroy, Martin, and Gebhard, *Sexual Behavior in the Human Female* (Philadelphia: W. B. Saunders Co., 1953), p. 293.

[4] *Ibid.*, p. 287.

18

riage, he claimed. On the basis of what he believed to be the widespread practice of promiscuity, Kinsey suggested a realignment of sexual values to cohere with public practice.[5] There have always been those of the "morality by nose count" school.

Billy Wilder's movies have overturned all the sexual mores, glorified promiscuity, glamorized prostitution, and elevated adultery to a virtue. Contrast Wilder's films such as "The Apartment" and "Irma La Douche" with the treatment of sexual deviation in Fellini's "La Dolce Vita." The saccharine sweet life of sexual dissipation is shown in this Italian film for the self-destructive delusion that it is.

Again *Playboy* magazine with its 300,000 plus circulation chiefly in the 18-30 age, single-male bracket trumpets sexual promiscuity and seduction of the innocent as the male ideal.

[5] See chapters 10 and 13, *Sexual Behavior in the Human Male;* William Graham Cole, *Sex in Christianity and Psychoanalysis* (New York: Oxford University Press, 1955), pp. 288, 317; *Sex Habits of American Men,* ed. Deutsch (New York: Prentice-Hall, Inc., 1948), p. 176. See also chapter 8, *Sexual Behavior in the Human Female.*

19

Women are bunnies to be fondled, kept, used. The girl is no more than a playboy accessory. Sex is to be enjoyed wherever one can steal it without the encumbrance of responsibility or loyalty of any kind. If she wants to tie you up or talk about marriage, run, rogue-male, run.

"The Playboy Philosophy," which one army man described as a phony attempt to give academic status to a girlie magazine, seems to advocate free sexual relationships between adults as long as there is a measure of responsibility and no coercion. Again, Hefner seems to insist that the marriage bond be respected. But the cartoons, jokes, and advice to the lovelorn in *Playboy* completely contradict this. Adultery is as much good clean fun as fornication. Like James Bond, the subtle and at times not so subtle insistence is upon the seduction of the nude, bosomy female. One letter to the *Playboy* advisor in the July, 1965, issue reads:

Nearly all the girls we date at our Midwestern college are fine where the physical aspects of love are concerned, but they lack the brain power necessary to make stimulating partners on other

20

levels. Although we place a high value on sensual satisfaction we feel there should be a sound intellectual relationship as well. Any suggestions?

Playboy's answer:

Since you'll never make your girls intellectual, . . . why don't you reverse your technique—and try *making* intellectual girls?

Another such letter in August of 1965 describes the guilt feelings of a young lad who had followed *Playboy's* advice. It seems he had removed a twenty-year-old girl's sexual reluctance (she had been raped at fourteen), had aroused her inner fire, and now the blaze was a runaway. He had turned the former prude into a profligate. Now she was "shacking up" with practically everybody on the campus and had gained a bad reputation. What could he do?

Playboy's answer:

Don't blame yourself. You did Sue a favor by helping her overcome a serious emotional shock.

The overall tone of *Playboy* is clear; it promotes the "manly art of seduction."

In other words, these contemporary voices

speak out for promiscuity. They would have us believe:

1. Every woman is waiting and wanting to be seduced.

2. Man is primarily an animal with a sexual drive, a drive which must be satisfied with anybody, any type, married or single.

I'm not sure whether these hot-blooded males and weak-kneed women are more to be pitied than censured or horselaughed into place. But certainly such a view of sexual relationships, of love and procreation, of human personality and potential, is warped and self-destructive, to say the least.

What about this assumption that all women are waiting and wanting to be seduced? Margaret Mead has suggested this to be a laughable period piece which belongs with mastodons, saber-tooth tigers, and pea-brain cave men pulling their women around by the hair. No self-respecting woman in these days is going to be treated like a playboy accessory, a cardigan sweater to be put in mothballs and placed on the shelf when not in use. Sexuality is far more deeply rooted in human personality than that. Certainly this assumption is belittling to women, an assumption to be deplored by the liberated ladies of the mid-twentieth century. Such male profligacy in the ancient world went hand in hand with the inferior position of women who were little more than expendable mattresses for the male animal. It has often been said that one of Christianity's great contributions to western society has been the elevation of women and children to a place of dignity and reverence. This came part and parcel with a Christian sex ethic which gave women and children a personal importance alongside men. Women could not be treated as sexual chattels or easily put off by divorce. They had rights and privileges of their own. The unwanted children of illicit relations could not be tossed in the ditch to die of cold or hunger. They too had rights and privileges. Thank God for the progress. With the increase of birth control methods, of course, the risk of unwanted children is lessened, but the inferior attitude toward women and children characteristic of promiscuity prevails.

23

Sexual promiscuity also belittles the male. Here man is assumed to be an irrational creature of undisciplined drives, little more than a sexual animal with the hunger to copulate. Under the lens of common sense we see this as a far less than adequate view of man. Some have suggested that the male rogue, *Playboy*-Bond approach to women is really antisexual, perhaps homosexual in a latent way.[6] For when men want to use women only as bunnies and accessories, thus running away from responsible sexual involvement, there is something basically wrong. Psychoanalysis recognizes that promiscuous sexual behavior springs from a disturbed personality.

But maturity demands sexual behavior that is motivated by respect for persons, the other party as well as one's self.

In contrast to this pagan drift toward promiscuity, consider the biblical view of man. In Genesis 1:27-28, 31, we read:

[6] See James M. Wall, "James Bond: Hero of Death and Destruction," *The Christian Advocate*, July 15, 1965, pp. 11-12.

So God created man in his own image, in the image of God he created him; male and female he created them. And God blessed them, and God said to them, "Be fruitful and multiply . . . ." And God saw everything that he had made, and behold, it was very good.

The biblical view of man affirms that our sexual differences and drives are given by God. God has made us male and female so that we may find joyful fulfillment in sexual union and the procreation of children. As a part of God's creation sex is good. The sexual organs are as much a part of God's handiwork as the eyes and ears of man. As the God-given sexual drive is what relates us to other people and opens the door to community, it is one of God's greatest gifts. In this we rejoice. There's nothing wrong with the appreciation of handsome physical proportions in either a man or a woman. God made us to enjoy them. Sometimes the church has failed to rejoice in God's creation of the human body. You remember Michelangelo's glorious painting of the creation on the ceiling of the Sistine Chapel in the Vatican. All the figures are in the nude as God created them. But then the artist's papal patron thought this indecent. He required clothes be painted on. Pope Julius II had his due reward, however, when Michelangelo painted the last judgment at the end of the chapel. The artist painted him in hell! We should rejoice in God's gift of sexual drives and differences. The biblical view of sex rejects both prudery and asceticism. *But once we think of persons only as physical, or begin to think of exploiting their bodies without concern for the whole person, then we are in trouble.* Such exploitation is possible in a beauty contest as well as in a bedroom. Man has a way of misusing the good things of God's creation, of diverting sex from its intended course so that its misuse destroys community and harms the self. So on the other extreme the biblical view of man rejects pornography and libertinism.

The Christian sex ethic with a biblical base may be expressed by four "R's": reverence, relatedness, responsibility, and renewal.

1. God calls us to reverence in our sexual life. God made and loves every human being; Christ died to redeem every child of man; therefore every person, male and female, is sacred. In I Corinthians 3:16, we read:

Do you not know that you are God's temple and that God's Spirit dwells in you? If any one destroys God's temple, God will destroy him. For God's temple is holy, and that temple you are.

Every individual must be treated as an end rather than a means or an accessory to an end. Another person is not just a "thing," an "it," a sexual organ or function to be used quite apart from the rest of his personality. Even a prostitute tries to protect her own dignity. Though she sells a sexual function, she specifically refuses to get involved as a person. Thus she can feel she has not given her self to be used as an accessory to someone else's pleasure. She has only sold a "function," not her self. Whether she or anyone can ever succeed in separating the sexual function from the rest of her *self* is doubtful. But that she

27

tries to, so as to see a certain difference in sold sex and the giving of her *self,* points to that certain reverence, dignity, self-acceptance for which we have been created.

Think about it. Don't you want to be treated as a person in your own right with feelings and needs of your own to be respected by others? Of course you do. Are you willing to treat your wife or husband this way, your date or fiancé? God calls us to see every human being as our "neighbor" and to love, to care, to reverence the neighbor. We are to be a Christ to our neighbor, said Luther, and that includes every potential sexual partner.

2. God calls us to relatedness in our sexual life. God created man and woman so that when they have sexual union they become one flesh:

Therefore a man leaves his father and his mother and cleaves to his wife, and they become one flesh. (Genesis 2:24.)

"This means that sexual union brings about the joining of two existences, economically, spiritually, and psychologically—and not just the union of two bodies. To attempt the one without the other is dangerous to the entire relationship." [7] Sexual compatibility and satisfaction between a couple involves the blending of mind and attitude as well as bodily contact. Helmut Thielicke has indicated the very difference between male and female "readiness," for sexual relationship requires a concern for the other person in order to achieve one's own fulfillment. Physical compatibility requires spiritual compatibility. Animal copulation is merely an instinctual, physical functioning. Human sexual relationships require a mutual concern and communication. [8]

Also guilt feelings and previous bad experiences can sour the relationship one wants to be most meaningful and genuine. Thielicke insists there is a monogamous physical nature in a woman since "she is the one who receives, the one who gives herself and participates with her

[7] William Graham Cole, *Sex in Christianity and Psychoanalysis* (New York: Oxford University Press, 1955), p. 297.

[8] Helmut Thielicke, *The Ethics of Sex* (New York: Harper and Row, 1964), p. 48.

whole being." She is marked by the first man who "possesses" her—"a girl never forgets her first love," as the old saying goes. It is to the polygamous male's interest to guard the monogamous female's self so that the female can give herself unreservedly to the male who desires her fully and finally.[9]

For sexual experience to mean the most, there must be a willingness for each to relate to the other with all candor, care, and concern. This rules out promiscuity.

3. God calls us to responsibility in our sexual life. If love means anything, it means loyalty. Remember again, "A man leaves his father and his mother and cleaves to his wife. . . ." This word "cleave" is old English for adhere to, stick to. It means that a couple are glued together. In societies where marriages are arranged, the loyalty comes first and the love comes later. Romantic love in our society can be a very superficial basis for sexual union because it may lack loyalty. Genuine love, giving ourselves completely to another person and re-

[9] *Ibid.*, p. 84.

ceiving his gift of self in return, requires trust and trustworthiness—cleaving to, glueing ourselves to another "for better for worse, for richer for poorer, in sickness and in health, to love and to cherish, till death us do part." How can we love someone for long whom we don't trust, someone who is unfaithful and dishonest with the deepest expression of our being? So a satisfying sexual union means we assume the responsibility for the feelings and affections of the other person, a responsibility for children which may result to the union, a responsibility toward the larger community—the protection of other couples, the protection of family property rights.

This is precisely why there are civil laws governing sexual union—to protect the wider community. And the marriage service of the churches frequently implies a responsibility to the community in the command, "If any man can show just cause why they may not lawfully be joined together, let him now speak, or else hereafter for ever hold his peace." Loyalty and community obligation can reduce the anxieties and insecurities which threaten a happy sexual

union. The promiscuous male or female who
trifles with the affections of others deserves to
be publicly censured. He or she is a criminal
threat to every other marriage and family on the
block, and hence a threat to a stable society.

Of course there are always some whose indiscretions have gotten them into trouble. They
are not to be condoned. For them there is,
however, the unique Christian message of renewal.

4. God calls us to renewal in our sexual life.
God will help each of us to begin again. Once
we have made our bed, we don't have to lie
in it. Every man and woman and all our relationships which we misuse for selfish reasons
can and must be renewed by the self-giving,
all-bearing, never-failing love of God. Pure lust
or even romantic love are quite inadequate for
an abiding relationship. So we must be renewed
by a richer, deeper, more responsible love such
as God has addressed toward us in Jesus Christ.
The scripture passage most frequently requested
by couples to be read at the marriage service is
the apostle Paul's hymn to Christlike love, the

thirteenth chapter of I Corinthians. Hear this portion of it:

Love is patient and kind; love is not jealous or boastful; it is not arrogant or rude. Love does not insist on its own way; it is not irritable or resentful; it does not rejoice at wrong, but rejoices in the right. Love bears all things, believes all things, hopes all things, endures all things.

As God has loved us in this way, so we can love others in this way with the help of his empowering presence within. As he forgives us, so we are enabled to forgive our marriage partner. As he bears all things and endures all things from us, so he can enable us to endure the temper tantrums and depressions of our spouse. Our lesser loves can take on the quality of his love defined in Jesus Christ. "Love one another," said Jesus, "even as I have loved you."

In the course of this chapter, I have insisted that the manly art of seduction is not manly at all. It is an escape from man's normal sexual role. Such sexual promiscuity belittles woman to the status of a mattress and belittles man to an irrational creature of appetites. Man's sexual

33

appetite must be directed and disciplined by the greater drive for meaning in his life. Christianity provides a system and source for our life's meaning. It rejoices in the sexual differences and drives given us by God. It insists that these differences and drives must be handled with reverence, relatedness, responsibility, and renewal. And all this points toward chastity before marriage and fidelity afterward. This age-old consensus still stands as the best ethical standard for modern sexual behavior.

One of the characters in Richard Llewellyn's *None but the Lonely Heart* observed, "I was out walking one day and in the distance I saw an animal. I came up closer and saw it was a man. I came up closer still and saw it was my brother." Here is the transition from pagan promiscuity to responsible Christian concern. Our fellowman is not an animal. God calls upon us to look upon our fellows as brothers and treat male and female as members of the family of God.

An attaché case with murder gimmicks, a .25 Beretta automatic with skeleton grip, a wire for strangling, a knife for slashing. A casual examination of this equipment would lead us to believe it belongs to a man of violence, perhaps a member of Murder, Inc. or the Ku Klux Klan. But those of you who have kept up on the movies and read the paperback thrillers of the past year will know these items identify Agent 007, James Bond, licensed to kill for patriotism and profit.

Mr. Bond is certainly not a peaceful man. He kills without compunction, without a second thought, and if he does not take joy in the infliction of pain, his

2
THE VIOLENT ONES

adversaries do. One of Ian Fleming's most frequently reprinted novels is appropriately called *Live and Let Die.* Two incidents from this particular title celebrate the pleasure of inflicting pain (that's one definition of sadism). One situation carefully described the way in which Mr. Big has Bond tortured by the slow doubling back of his little finger until it cracks and our hero faints with a soft animal groan. On another occasion CIA friend Felix Leiter is fed to the sharks. What is left of Leiter is piled mummy-like in the corner with a penciled note left in his mouth: "He disagreed with something that ate him."

The *Goldfinger* movie has a sizzling beginning. Bond is making red-hot advances to a pretty young thing in her boudoir when she sets him up for a mugging from the rear. With all the skill of his commando training, Bond flips the hood over his shoulder and into milady's tubful of bath water. Then our invincible hero throws the live electric heater into the tub with the uninvited guest, and we are treated to the deep fry of an instant electrocution. *From*

Russia, with Love opens with the stalking and strangling of a James Bond stand-in at the Smersh gardens training center. The poor stunt man stand-in wearing a J. B. false face really gets it for good with a wire garrote. And we the public get to view every tense, vicious moment of it.

Why is this sadistic stuff popular? Why can magazines sell more magazines with pictures of the gruesome and vicious than those of the sweet and serene? What about the demand for violence on television? Doesn't this say something about the sickness of society, a sickness with whose germs we are all infected? One editor has suggested that James Bond is a contemporary hero of death and destruction, *popular because of our own preference for death and destruction over life and love.*[1]

The accent on violence is not new in our society. Violence has been a part of our young nation's life from the beginning. The tradition

[1] James M. Wall, "James Bond: Hero of Death and Destruction," *The Christian Advocate,* July 15, 1965, p. 11.

37

of every man settling his own disputes with his fists or his six-gun on the early frontier or in today's streets is all too familiar to us. A number of our presidents have been assassinated, but the public is unwilling to limit its possession of firearms. Harrison Salisbury writing in his book on juvenile delinquency, *The Shook-Up Generation,* quotes a California criminologist on a trend in the nation as a whole toward more and more vicious violence. "The accent on violence is expressed many ways," he says,

the use of atomic power for mass destruction in warfare, overpowerful motor vehicles, acute international tensions implying the threat of war, intense racial tensions, etc. These developments are enforced by mass communication media which are more suggestive and impressive than ever before— television programs which can be observed at home, day and night, motion pictures, emphasizing and actually glorifying violence as indicative of masculinity, gory newspaper reports as well as comic strips and comic books which feature force and ridicule higher values.[2]

[2] (Greenwich, Conn.: Fawcett Publications, Inc., 1958), p. 163.

Is this overstated? Well, go into the dime store and check the toys available for children. You can get a machine-gun-like contraption for Junior. It shoots whistling grenades, fires rapid-fire bullets, and has a detachable pistol for close rapid fire. "All the sound and fury a boy could want," says the ad. I suppose the children play at murdering Chinese-Negroes, or the neighbor family in their sleep, or Vietnamese villagers who might be Viet Cong. The attaché case contains a booby trap or a hidden dagger— all your little tot needs for fun and games. It's ironic, isn't it, the way Santa Claus brings models of death and destruction to our children on the birthday of the Prince of Peace. If the John Birch Society wants a real subverter of the public good, they ought to investigate Santa Claus. He does wear a red suit, you know.

Of course many have argued that toy weapons and creep shows for kids do no harm whatsoever. Kids have always played soldiers, cowboys, and Indians. In his novel *Dr. Zhivago*, Boris Pasternak described two boys "playing the most terrible and adult of games, war;

39

moreover, participation in this particular war was punishable by deportation and hanging." Yet the way their woolen caps were tied at the back suggested that they still had fathers and mothers who looked after them. "Their dangerous amusements," said Pasternak, *"had a bloom of innocence that they communicated to everything. . . ."* I wonder. Where does the bloom of innocence stop and the fall from innocence begin? If all this playacting of violence in our culture is not damaging, why the crowds in the streets yelling "jump, jump" to the poor troubled creatures on the rooftops? Why the violence in the streets of Selma, Saigon, and Los Angeles? Of course there are many reasons, but could not one of them be this genial acceptance, this open predisposition toward violent means to settle differences?

Some of you may have seen the German movie entitled "The Bridge," introduced to American audiences by Chet Huntley. Widely seen in contemporary Germany, it was a story about some high-school boys in a small German town at the close of the Second World War.

They had been too young to serve in the army, but how they longed to be soldiers for the glory of the fatherland! Then at the last minute these wide-eyed kids were conscripted and with a day's training were ordered to hold a bridge in the town from advancing American troops while the German regulars retreated. It all started as a wonderful game but ended in a bloody tragedy. All but one of the boys were killed, and the bridge wasn't really important after all. Chet Huntley suggested the film raised questions about the danger of militarism in a dictatorship.

Is there a growing preference in this nation "for death and destruction over life and love"? Have we substituted "Live and Let Die" for "Live and Let Live"? With the systematic military training of our young men to be masters of violence, and the violence in the mass media, have we accepted this as a normal course for the settling of differences? One of the questions Art Linkletter asked of a little girl in a "House-party" interview some time ago was, "Should we go to the moon?" "Oh, yes," said the child, "we must destroy them before they destroy us."

41

What are our simple military solutions, our resorts to violence doing to our children? Have we lost the ability to love, the ability to negotiate, cooperate, and participate?

To this violent, shook-up generation, the Bible commends a more excellent way than the way of violence. It is the way of Christlike love. The apostle Paul described this love in his thirteenth chapter of I Corinthians:

Love is patient and kind; love is not jealous or boastful; it is not arrogant or rude. Love does not insist on its own way; it is not resentful; it does not rejoice at wrong, but rejoices in the right. Love bears all things, believes all things, hopes all things, endures all things.

God is patient with *homo sapiens,* this funny little quadruped he raised on hind feet with a self-consciousness and a higher destiny, *patient and kind* with man's slow and arduous evolution toward decency and dignity. There was Calvary, and the Inquisition, and the Salem witch trials, Auschwitz's stinking ovens, and bloody Hayneville, Alabama. But God is patient and kind.

Our Lord Jesus Christ was not *jealous or boast-ful*, for "though he was in the form of God, [he] did not count equality with God a thing to be grasped, but emptied himself, taking the form of a servant, being born in the likeness of men. And being found in human form he humbled himself and became obedient unto death, even death on a cross" (Phil. 2:6-8). Our Lord *was not arrogant or rude*—he called us to the royalty of service which he followed himself. Instead of a scepter and crown he took a basin and towel as the symbols of his ministry—and a cross came to symbolize his life. *"Love does not insist on its own way"*—he certainly did not: "not my will, but thine be done." Can we rejoice at wrong in his presence? Can we be glad when others go wrong? No, like the patient, forgiving father we will rejoice when the prodigal comes home. A father said to his teen-age daughters: "Remember, girls, whatever you do you can always come home." We will not be glad when others go wrong—we will rejoice in the right. Such a love revealed in Jesus Christ and present in each of us, if we

43

would but give him heed, "bears all things, believes all things, hopes all things, endures all things." What a wonderful possibility for each of us, to be filled with and obedient to this Christlike love of God—to love others even as he first loved us. This is the way more excellent than violence for modern man.

Some have argued that this way of love is merely an interim ethic, a utopian pipe dream inapplicable to the problems of our technical, urban society. *But the way of love, the concern for others, is far more applicable to our common life than we have tried.* Love would have us *negotiate* our disputes in industry, international affairs, and family life rather than resort to violence. Negotiation takes more patience and kindness, less arrogance and jealousy, more courage and endurance, than violence. Warren Austin, former U.S. Ambassador to the United Nations, once characterized this world body as the place where diplomats get ulcers so that young soldiers won't have to get bullets. Love would have us *cooperate* in the common social challenges before us, the hopefully nonviolent war on poverty and prejudice, for example. Here are problems for the rich and the poor, the white and the black to tackle together. We have surely learned in our northern and western cities that nonviolence will become violence if we do not take the initiative to cooperate for the common good. Could the Watts riots in Los Angeles have been prevented by intelligent good will over the years? Love would have the strong *participate* in the causes of the weak, would have us become involved in community life. "I don't want to get involved." "I don't want to be responsible." Do you want to be irresponsible? The Christian is involved in the crises and cares of humanity.

Let me quickly add that our willingness to love, to negotiate, cooperate, and participate provides no simple solutions, but neither does violence. Love at least does respect persons enough that it *will not* kill them, abuse them, manipulate them for the sake of abstract principles like national self-interest, or white superiority, or economic individualism. Love *wants* to keep people alive and growing, working and

45

playing, and is willing to suffer every indignity and pay every cost to make this possible. As a last resort and with admission of sin, violence may be necessary, wars may be defined as just, self-defense and police protection will restrain the evildoer. But James Bond as a hero symbol celebrates and glorifies unnecessary violence. Remember, "while we were yet sinners . . . Christ died for us." Christlike love would have us swallow our pride and toughen our hide to stay at the bargaining table, endure the committee work, endure the misunderstanding and resentment, to give of our time and money that violence may be avoided, persons helped, and community achieved.

So we insist the Christian ethic is fully as practical, and more so, than violence. The question is, is sinful man, as we know ourselves to be, able to live for others in this way? Christians should be the first to admit they lack the motivation and capacity to love and be loved like Christ, unless they receive this help from God. The human heart is a pretty hard cookie which must be softened. It is a hard core of exag-

46

gerated self-interest which must be humanized or christianized to care for others. The *motivation* for Christlike love to others is that God has first loved us through Christ. We love others because he first loved us. Furthermore, the Christian knows that *God is present in him.* We speak of this personal presence of God as the Holy Spirit. God is present in us to help us love others as we have been loved by God. So what is impossible for man—to negotiate, to cooperate, to participate—is possible with God's help. This is certainly what our Lord said when his students wondered how man might be saved—according to the terms he taught: "What is impossible with men, is possible with God" (Luke 18:27).

Actually Christianity rises or falls on the proposition that a new humanity in the individual and society is possible. Christians tend to be quite pessimistic and realistic about man, but optimistic and hopeful about God.

A new orientation and motivation for individuals and for society is possible where men and movements will accept the love of God in

47

Christ and be obedient to him. Man will continually resort to violence. Yes! But God and man can overcome this escape from responsibility. *Full humanity and concern for others is possible when God softens our hard hearts and warms them with love for others.*

Compare these instruments of violence—a Beretta, wire, and knife, a zip gun, an army automatic—with these instruments of love: representatives of management and labor negotiating a new steel contract, the U.N. General Assembly addressed by Pope Paul who echoes the eloquent encyclical of John XXIII, "Peace on Earth," the cooperation of white and Negro youth in the Peace Corps, a church work camp rebuilding bombed out southern churches. Which of these offers our true hope for the future?

One of America's great primitive painters was the Quaker Edward Hicks. He loved to paint a subject he entitled "The Peaceable Kingdom." Indeed, he did more than seventy-five different canvasses of this particular theme. All the paintings portray the biblical theme of hope and

48

longing for true community in nature, red with tooth and claw, and in human relations, so stained and streaked with violence. The prophet Isaiah had looked forward to that day when God would reign over his people through a messiah of righteousness and faithfulness. Then, says Isaiah,

the leopard shall lie down with the kid, and the calf and the lion and the fatling together, . . . the lion shall eat straw like the ox. The sucking child shall play over the hole of the asp. . . . *They shall not hurt or destroy in all my holy mountain; for the earth shall be full of the knowledge of the Lord as the waters cover the sea.* (Isaiah 11:6-9.)

This is not just prophet, poet, painter's fancy for a future never-never land. In the lower portion of these canvasses we see William Penn standing under a great Pennsylvania oak, negotiating with the Indians for the sale of their lands to the white colonists. Hicks saw this early American effort at negotiation, rather than theft, rape, and murder, the triplets of violence, to be

49

a very practical sign that the peaceable kingdom is already here in part. God's reign is
present wherever men love others because he
first loved us—wherever men sweat and strive
to negotiate, cooperate, and participate for the
common good, for true community. God grant
that we may find our place in his peaceable
kingdom.

3
SNOBBERY MADE SIMPLE

James Bond, Ian Fleming's popular secret agent 007, is a brand dropper. Though Bond comes from a lowbrow background, he has acquired aristocratic tastes. He knows how to move in highbrow circles —to order the proper wine of the best vintage year of the most exclusive label all appropriate to a properly ordered meal. He has really arrived. His clothes, his cars, his hand-made cigarettes all have snob appeal. Perhaps Bond is popular because all this appeals to our affluent society.

Name-dropping, place-dropping, celebrity-collecting are other facets of the snobbery syndrome. A famous playwright's grandmother was characterized as a snob who took her exercise picking up celebrities and dropping their names. "Her life" (really an interesting one), says the playwright's biographer, "was a string of diamonds which she managed to turn into costume jewelry."

Look at advertising. El Ropo is an aristocratic smoke. If you're going to die prematurely of mouth cancer, you might as well go in style. Be sure and have caviar at your bridge party. You may hate those slimy fish eggs, but it sure will show the girls you have arrived. And be sure you've bought the right label, the drink of distinction. What car will you drive? Rising young executives drive Thunderbirds. Of course only rising young executives can afford Thunderbirds. Are you attracted by the real-estate ads which describe their product in fancy French phrases, which speak of an "exclusive neighborhood" and an "estate-size lot," which appeal to an executive-type buyer? You know we no longer sleep in a bedroom—we rest in a "sleeping chamber." The living room has become a "reception galleria." This kind of advertising is snob appeal, pure and simple.

The advertiser is not the culprit to be con-
demned. He reflects something in each one of
us and in our society. Neither am I singling
out a person for enjoying quality food, clothes,
car, or house. You may very much enjoy caviar
from the Black Sea, Sea Island shirts, Bentley-
Continental motor cars, and be able to pay for
them, without being a snob. But whenever food,
clothes, cars, and even knowledge become a
pose, a claim of superiority, a cause for conde-
scending to those inferior to us or bootlicking
those supposed superior—then life is out of
joint. According to Webster, the snob is "one
who blatantly imitates, fawningly admires, or
vulgarly seeks association with those he regards
as his superiors." "A snob," said Somerset
Maugham, "would put up with any affront . . .
would ignore any rebuff . . . would swallow any
rudeness to get asked to a party he wanted to
go to." There are academic snobs who assume
the Ph.D. is the only guarantee of good teaching.
And then among the Ph.D.'s there is a priority
among the schools where you studied. There
are clothes snobs who feel quite superior about

the styles and brand names they wear. They are real anxious for you to know. The *Status Seekers,* says Vance Packard, "are people who are continually straining to surround themselves with visible evidence of the superior rank they are claiming." [1] They strain to have the proper address, the proper friends, clubs, and churches, the proper diploma and political party. Like the Kwatkuitl Indians of North America, they strain toward a certain conspicuous consumption, being big spenders and tippers—as an indication of their superior status.

The British Broadway musical, "Stop the World, I Want to Get Off," is a modern morality play about the seven ages of man. The central character is a modern Everyman by the name of Littlechap. His frantic search for sex, status, and success represents every one of us and the drift of our society today. Early in his life Littlechap sets his goal for personal achievement as he sees it in the culture about him. He sings about wanting to be rich with all the clothes, cars, and affluent connections money can buy.

[1] (New York: Pocket Books, Inc., 1961), p. 5.

This will impress the ladies and get his face in the papers. To be "dirty, rotten, filthy, stinking rich," to "mix with the nobs" and sit with the snobs—that's the life for me.

Well, Littlechap works hard and becomes just what he had hoped to be—a rich snob. Several times throughout his life there are moments of crisis which threaten to crack his phoniness, moments when he seems to ask himself some basic questions about the meaning of it all, the purpose of his life. With the death of his first son, the threat of a world war, he runs to the edge of the stage and cries, "Stop the world, this rat-race social pace I've been living in." But each time before he can seriously face up to himself, he tells a little joke or makes the small talk we frequently engage in to evade the big talk about important things. Then quickly he is back in his phony, rat-race world again.

Finally toward the end of his life, after his wife has died, he at last faces up to himself. He realizes how he never really gave himself to his wife and children. He has only used them, as everyone else in his life, for his own selfish advantage. Thus at the end of his life he is no longer singing: "I wanta be rich," he is singing another tune: "What kind of fool am I?"

We may not all manifest the same marks of snobbery, but there is an awful lot of straining and striving in our American life which touches most of us somewhere. We are never happy with what we have, our luxuries become our necessities, we envy the rank above us. Think of the ways we step on others of another color, culture, religion, or language so as to give ourselves more class. We don't run down the Negro American, the Latin American, the Indian American, the Japanese American primarily because of their different color, culture, or language. That would be un-American, unpatriotic. No, one of the basic reasons we run down minority groups is to enable our own desperate grasp for status. We assume we can give our own pathetic personalities more class, running up our own status by running down somebody else's. Segregation is really a kind of legalized or organized status. Deep down, it assumes we cannot be somebodies on our own unless we can make others into nobodies by comparison. Certainly this is contrary to every person-centered concern of the Christian ethic.

The ways we climb are pretty obvious and the sociologist can describe them for us. One way to picture the situation graphically, says Vance Packard, is to picture our society as a high mountain everybody is trying to climb. At the bottom of the mountain there is room for a lot of people. Less and less people can crowd to the top. The pinnacle is a pretty exclusive club. But why do we climb? This is the question that gets at motivation. Why is there this anxious worrying and scurrying to move up the social ladder, to get to the top of the social heap, to be what we are not in superficial terms? Do we climb the mountain simply because it is there, as some mountaineers have put it? Or does our social adventuring express a God-given aspiration toward fulfillment, excellence, maturity in every human being? Is the mountain out there or in here? Is the challenge to conquer, to excel on the outside or within each one of us?

There is a built-in drive for completion in all living things. Seed, shoot, and stalk show this growth toward completion. We see this drive to develop in the fledgling bird which inevitably leaves the security of the nest to try his wings in the vast abyss of the air. Birds cannot remain nestlings. They must become masters of the sky. Some of you may have seen a pine tree growing from the crevice of a rock in mountain country. It lodged there as a seed and began to grow. As it grew, this inner determination to develop eventually widened the crevice and split the rock in two. There is such an inner drive toward maturity and excellence in man. We all search for health, wholeness, and holiness. All three words come from the same Anglo-Saxon root word *hal*—a word used to point toward a concept of integrated fulfillment of man's potential. What man is seeking, often unconscious and all unaware, is authentic manhood, a genuinely human existence. Furthermore, we must *understand that God is working toward this goal of our maturity within each one of us*. We speak of this presence

58

of God working in us as the Holy Spirit. As a physician assists at the birth of a child, so the Holy Spirit is ever assisting us in the flowering of our personality. A genuine human existence is God's goal for every man.

But snobbery and status-seeking is a perversion of this quest. Someone has suggested the origin of the word "snob" to be in the abbreviation "s. nob." It stood for *sine nobilitas,* without nobility. In this sense, then, the snob is one who aspires to prominence without character. He pursues his perfection in the wrong direction—in the superficial, skin-deep status symbols of society. He wants distinction without any genuine depth.

Now if we honestly see ourselves, each of us inevitably involved in this worrisome business of keeping up with and ahead of the Joneses, and if we realize this outward frenzy to climb the ladder of class is a perversion of an inward drive to grow in character, then half our battle is won. Now we are ready to talk about where this inward thrust *is* leading us and how we shall be helped to get there. *The Bible has a great deal to say to us about the nature and destiny of man.* The Bible recognizes this inner drive for perfection, this hunger for fullness of life. Indeed, our Lord Jesus Christ insisted that he had come that we might have life and have it more abundantly. (John 10:10.) Actually the word "perfection" as the goal of man is used nineteen times in the New Testament. This Greek word is *teleios* which means full-grown, mature, having reached the appointed end of one's development. To be without flaw or blemish, a frozen ideal, is one kind of perfection I am sure we could never achieve. But to grow up, to mature toward what God has created us to be, this is a possibility we must keep ever before us. There is a potential deep within us yearning to be completed.

In Ephesians the apostle Paul describes God's many gifts to the church, a diversity of gifts to fulfill many different ministries. But all are given that this people shall grow to "mature manhood, to the measure of the stature of the fullness of Christ" (Ephesians 4:13). "We are to grow up in every way into him who is the head, into Christ" (Ephesians 4:15). You see, each of us is called to complete our manhood or womanhood. What a tragedy it is to see people who never grow up, who are petty and peevish and childish when they are at a physical age quite beyond their childhood. A New York police chief was asked by a P.T.A. member for his advice to teen-agers. He said,

Go home. Hang the storm windows. Paint the woodwork. Shovel the walk, wash the car. Learn to cook. Scrub the floors. Repair the sink. Build a boat. Get a job. . . . Help the minister, the priest or rabbi; the Red Cross, the Salvation Army. . . . Study your lessons. And then, when you are through and not tired, read a book. In plain, simple words: grow up, quit acting like a crybaby, get out of your dream world; start acting like a man or lady.[2]

The remedy for a lot of teen-age violence against persons and property is to "grow up." But then again a lot of adults need to grow up.

What does it mean to be grown up and mature, to be perfected? The Ephesians passage

[2] *Voices of Protest and Hope*, compiled by Elizabeth D. Dodds (New York: Friendship Press, 1965), p. 141.

just quoted says the measure of our manhood or womanhood is to be found in Jesus Christ. The physical height of a child is frequently measured by a scale of ascending marks on the kitchen door. But the measure of our human maturity is found on no kitchen door, on no physical scale. Matthias Grünewald, a Reformation artist of the sixteenth century, painted the measure of our manhood. He painted a man for others. He painted a scene of public execution, a grisly canvas full of tortured muscles, torn flesh, and frenzied painful hands, a man on a cross as big as life, a man who laid down his life for his enemies. A man who said to the climbers and strainers, "Father, forgive them for they know not what they do." He painted a man who has said, "Why be so anxious about your own life? Submit yourself to God's authority and his righteousness first, and these other things will fall into place." Aim for heaven, and earth will be thrown in. He painted a man so secure in God's acceptance that he was freed to be fully human, freed from anxiety about himself, freed to love and trust other human beings.

At the side of the cross stands John the Baptist, surely an anachronism at the crucifixion, but in the Gospels he had been the forerunner of Jesus crying out in those years before, "Behold, the Lamb of God, who takes away the sin of the world!" Now he stands as God's sentinel in history and points with elongated finger to this great man on the cross as if to say to us, "O you climbers and strainers, there is the man for others you are meant to be."

The social-climbing standards of this passing age are folly in God's sight and should be in ours. For class without character is superficial and impermanent. It will not satisfy the deep hungers within us for perfection, for maturity. So instead of "putting on the dog" and playing the snob, God calls us to put on the Lord Jesus Christ. The words of the apostle Paul may well be your words of commitment now:

Not that I have already obtained this or am already perfect; but I press on . . . toward the goal for the prize of the upward call of God in Christ Jesus. (Philippians 3:12, 14.)

Make Christ your goal and press on.

The leisure-time revolution is here. "It is the gravest crisis ahead for American Society," said one of our foremost news commentators on an end-of-the-year television program looking into the future. How can this great increase in leisure time be a dangerous threat? For most people it looks too good to be true. But the gift of free time, time for leisure, may be a blessing or a curse, depending on how people use it. To some it can bring abiding joy and life fulfillment. On the other hand free time may lead to boredom, stagnation, and suicide for increasing numbers of our early retirees. For the affluent it can lead to deca-

4
THE
PLEASURE
SEEKERS

dence and delinquency, for adult and juvenile alike.

James Bond, whom we have taken as a reflection of a changing world of values, fills his leisure hours with fun time. He is one of the new breed of pleasure seekers—not that pleasure is a new pursuit, but the means of pursuit are far more ingenious today. Bond loves to gamble for big stakes, and his expense-account job enables him to jump from continent to continent, casino to casino. Baccarat seems to be his favorite game, but he is equally adept at cards, golf, and scissors-cut-paper. On all of them he is willing to gamble a wallet and cheat to win. Mr. Bond is also a drinking man who is willing to take on any bottle from rotgut to the bonded best. He's fond of sports cars, proud of his racing change, and willing to consider every driver on the road his competitor. At other times you might think Bond's god is his belly, for he loves to eat and is very particular about what and where he eats.

James Bond's fun time is devoted to gambling, guzzling, gunning, gourmandism. These pleasure pursuits are no longer just the sports of kings, wealthy playboys, and the jet set. They are within the reach of many. With the increase of affluence and leisure, John Doe can blow a little, and possibly a lot, of his ready cash on Saturday night poker or a weekend in Las Vegas. He can stock his own liquor cabinet and join the cocktail set. He can buy a little sports car and drag off for the rally. Credit cards have made great fun out of restaurant hopping. Feed now and finance later. The beaches are crowded, the lakes are crammed. Culture and cookouts are big business.

This is great, and many of us need a fun break. Fun, in its proper perspective, we all need! But there are signs of a new hedonism, the pursuit of pleasure as an end in itself, as the chief measure of man's meaning. If pleasure becomes the *summum bonum,* the highest good, the pursuit of happiness may get out of hand. "Can we survive the fun explosion?" asked Joseph Wood Krutch sometime ago.[1] Are leisure time and resources meant to be conspicuously

[1] *The Saturday Review,* January 16, 1965, pp. 14-16.

consumed for the titillation of one's own nerve ends? Is life meant to be a perpetual Coney Island? Must everything be measured for kicks? In an earlier day, clocks were fashioned by monks to awaken them at 4 A.M. to say their prayers. Today we watch the clock for coffee breaks and fun times. From prayer time to play time, we've come a long way. There has been a change in our sense of values. We have been led to think we are entitled to a "fun time" in every hour and a sexpot in every bedroom. We are encouraged to "express ourselves," to do what comes naturally without training or restraint. Eat, drink, be merry—it's later than you think. Pleasure for pleasure's sake is the apparent premise for many. But will this premise stand the test of common sense, let alone the test of the Christian ethic?

Remember the words of Richard Rogers' official song for the New York World's Fair: "Walk away from every care . . ." ?

Attractive on the surface, isn't it? But have you compared it with the *theme* of the World's Fair: "Man's Achievements in an Expanding

Universe"? The song and the theme are completely contradictory, aren't they? Man's achievements depend upon someone having cared. Who will care if having fun is foremost? Who says we are entitled to it, to eat without work, to rights without responsibilities, to take from the till, without contributing our share? Who will slaughter the hogs, bake the bread, and dip the candles, be the butcher, the baker, the candlestick maker? Who will reflect on the wisdom of the past and seek to settle the problems of the present? Who will bear the burdens of human need? The pleasure seekers? The fun-oriented? The pleasure seekers seem to assume that security and abundance are permanent and automatic. We know this simply isn't so. Human progress comes by inspiration and perspiration, by millions of unknown people doing their little thankless jobs with faithfulness and perseverance in the hope of a better day. Hedonism is weighed in the balance over against man's desire to achieve, and is found wanting.

Joseph Wood Krutch has suggested that such hedonism may lead to despair and violence.

The swells on the richer side of the tracks push for kicks day and night, something different, something new. The mods and rockers in the inner city also assume life is just a bowl of cherries. When the director of Friendship House in Lambuth Borough, London, asked his young toughs what they wanted out of life, they replied, "Money, booze, and girls." Well, what happens when the money, booze, and girls run out? They will sometime. And the body gets tired, the spirit becomes depressed. Like a narcotic, the pursuit of pleasure demands ever larger doses more ingeniously administered to return the same amount of "kicks." You can't have fun all the time. Frustration and boredom set in. For the thoughtful, such boredom and frustration may end in pessimism. For the unthoughtful, the inevitable result may be violence and rebellion. In our pleasure-seeking age there is a high incidence of violence and suicide. The age of fun is also the age of vandalism and philosophical despair. Could the pursuit of pleasure as the chief end of man be a contributing factor?

If then pleasure be so empty as the primary pursuit of a man's life, why are there so many suckers? Perhaps the pursuit of pleasure is a search for something far more profound and necessary than may be recognized. The frenzy for kicks in our time is a symptom of an over-anxious conscience, worried about saving the self. All of us are searching for meaning, for fulfillment, but many are seeking in the wrong place. We are trying to dig our gold in a washed-out mine, or worse yet, in a lead or salt mine that never had any gold.

Take *gambling*, for instance. The disturbing rise in public gambling points to the way many are filling their leisure hours. In 1964 more than sixty million Americans attended the horse races and wagered $4.3 billion. Many a gambler mistakenly searches for meaning in the dictates of chance. Some gamble casually, some compulsively, searching for a direction, a decision for their life in the turn of a card, the roll of the dice, the determination of a race.

Or *guzzling*. The great increase in social drinking and the rise of alcoholism as a modern disease is not just a tribute to the distiller's art of manufacturing and advertising. In these anxious, troubled days many search for meaning in the sparkle and sedation of a glass—sparkle and pizazz for tired spirits and empty minds, sedation and anesthesia for moral responsibility and genuine guilt.

Or *gunning*. The American love affair with the automobile as a status symbol, a plaything, an expression of freedom, and incidentally a means of transportation, may represent far more than these. It may represent our search for meaning in the mastery of the machine. We live in a machine age, when machines are rapidly replacing the functions of men. At least with the automobile we can prove our mastery, our superiority, the dominance of mind over mechanism. So we squeal our tires, gun our motor, grind the gears, and roar off down the highway trying to prove something about ourselves, and often at great risk to others.

And *gourmandism*. More Americans are eating out than ever before, searching out the unique and bizarre in taste-bud-tantalizers while much

71

of the rest of the human family set their envious and emaciated eyes upon the size of our garbage cans. Our skill with a menu, our fascination with good food may be a search for meaning in the cult of the calorie, the sophistication of physical survival. Our "eat to live" may have become our "live to eat."

In the pursuit of pleasure, in the frenzy for kicks many are searching for a fulfillment and meaning in their lives, all unaware that what they truly seek is beyond pleasure.

Where the sun shines in the street
There are very many feet
Seeking God, all unaware
That their hastening is a prayer.
Perhaps these feet would deem it odd
(Who think they are on "pleasure" bent)
If someone went,
And told them, "You are seeking God." [2]

The Westminster Catechism, formulated in the seventeenth century, begins with a question and answer still basic for modern man.

[2] Mary Carolyn Davies, "Feet." In the sixth line I have substituted "pleasure" for "business."

"Question: What is the chief and highest end of man? Answer: Man's chief and highest end is to glorify God, and fully to enjoy him forever." The New Testament speaks of a joy which may be ours, a joy in knowing and serving God, a joy which may be ours even in the midst of persecution and suffering. Listen to I Peter 1:3-6:

Blessed be the God and Father of our Lord Jesus Christ! By his great mercy we have been born anew to a living hope through the resurrection of Jesus Christ from the dead. . . . In this you rejoice, though now for a little while you may have to suffer various trials.

We hear the same note in the beatitudes of our Lord:

Blessed are the poor in spirit. . . .
Blessed are those who mourn. . . .
Blessed are the meek. . . .
Blessed are those who hunger and thirst for righteousness. . . .
Blessed are the merciful . . . the pure in heart . . . the peacemakers. . . .

73

Blessed are you when men revile you and persecute you and utter all kinds of evil against you falsely on my account.

Rejoice and be glad, for your reward is great in heaven, for so men persecuted the prophets who were before you. (Matthew 5:3-12.)

Persecution, war, hunger, mourning—life is like that—and yet blessedness in the midst of it all? How can this be?

Because God in his love accepts us just as we are for now and forever, the Christian is able to accept life joyfully as it comes, the bitter and the sweet, the blue and the gold. The Christian may not understand the tragic, but he knows this is not the whole story. He will not let his partial view warp his vision of the whole as being a good world from the hands of a gracious God. Because God accepts us, we can accept ourselves. Because God accepts us, we can accept others. And because God accepts us we can accept the universe, enjoy the infinite variety and marvel of God's vast creation. Bernard Kops, one of England's angry young men, has said something which sounds surprisingly like a modern St. Francis, God's troubadour:

Sing you silly sod! . . . Sing that a flower is a flower and the world is a wedding. Sing because we are. . . . Even if we are going to be annihilated that was no reason to die before we died. Sing to wake the living and the dead. Just sing. Say yes to life. Yes, yes, yes, and yes again.[3]

Like Zorba the Greek,[4] we can dance as well as sing, in time of tears and triumph, to celebrate the givenness and the goodness of life. So here is the blessedness beyond pleasure and happiness: a dependence on God and a joy in his presence and promises. Here in the service of God, the love of God, man finds a meaning and a fulfillment for his life, a joy and blessedness, deeper, richer, and more lasting than pleasure.

Now lest you think I have been knocking all fun and pleasure, let me insist that I have been setting *the Christian context* for all our

[3] "The World Is a Wedding," from *Voices of Protest and Hope*, compiled by Elisabeth D. Dodds (New York: Friendship Press, 1965), pp. 116-17.

[4] See the novel, or movie on the novel, by Nikos Kazantzakis.

work and play. Remember, the chief end of man is to glorify God and enjoy him forever. At the Interchurch Center in New York City there is an impressive wood sculpture in bas relief showing men and women engaged in various vocational and recreational pursuits. Beneath these vignettes of work and play are the words of the apostle Paul in I Corinthians 10:31, "Whether you eat or drink or whatever you do, do all to the glory of God." All our work, all our recreation must honor him. We honor him when we honor his creation, when we respect the elements, when we serve the well-being of man. Does your recreation really serve to recreate the body and mind God has given you—or do you wake up the morning after wishing the night before had never been? Do you use your leisure time for the service of others, for personal and community renewal, for cultural and educational enrichment, for the conservation and appreciation of God's good creation? Does your work and play fall in this bracket of glorifying God? The Protestant ethic has had a great deal to say about serving God

with and in our work. But in our day we must
consider how we may glorify God in our increased leisure time. God's acceptance enables
us to use our leisure time for the renewal of
man and the service of God. As we seek to
glorify him he grants us a blessedness beyond
pleasure and happiness.

The first time one goes to Coney Island it's a
fun thing. But after several trips it begins to
get cheap and gaudy, noisy and irritating, full
of tinsel and trash for cash. One could hardly
want to make a life of it, a continuous clatter
of chills, thrills, and spills. But when you look
away from the boardwalk, across the beach, you
face the sea. There you can always see people
on benches facing the vast wonder and mystery
of the ocean. There are young couples whis-
pering of their love and faith to each other,
discussing the promise of life before them. And
there are the aged reflecting on the past and
straining their eyes across that mystery before
them, hopeful of seeing a distant shore, a harbor
for their little craft, and home. Life is not
meant to be a perpetual Coney Island, an endless

pursuit of pleasure. Rather, it is a search for meaning in the midst of mystery. From Jesus Christ we have a clue as to the meaning of the mystery: "Seek first his kingdom and his righteousness, and all these things shall be yours as well" (Matthew 6:33). For you see, the chief end of man is to glorify God and enjoy him forever.

"The villains and the heroes get all mixed up," said James Bond from his hospital bed. The killing business used to be so simple, so clearly right or wrong. Bond is recuperating from the torture inflicted by Le Chiffre in the *Casino Royale* affair. Physically and emotionally depressed, he questions the morality of his secret-service job as a hired assassin. In so doing he reflects the moral confusion of our time. "Of course," says Bond, "patriotism comes along and makes it seem fairly all right [killing of the villain], but this country-right-or-wrong business is getting a little out of date. Today we are fighting Communism. Okay, If

5
FOR
LOVE
OF
COUNTRY

I'd been alive fifty years ago, the brand of conservatism we have today would have been damn near called Communism, and we should have been told to go and fight that. History is moving pretty quickly these days, and the heroes and villains keep on changing parts." [1]

Our American history certainly makes this clear. In 1754, Americans fought with the English against the French in the French and Indian War. In 1776 and 1812, we fought with the French against the English. In 1846, the United States went to war with Mexico on behalf of the southern state of Texas. In 1861, the southern state of Texas went to war against the United States north of the Mason-Dixon line. In 1898, America went to the rescue of Cuba against Spain. In 1961, Russia tried to go to the rescue of Cuba against America. By 1917, the First World War saw America, France, Britain join with Italy, Russia, and Japan fighting Germany. In the 1940's, Italy and Japan were our enemies—Russia was our friend. But within ten years, America was good friends with Ger-

[1] *Casino Royale,* pp. 109-10.

many and Italy and Japan, and Russia is now our enemy. Agent 007 was right. The villains and heroes do get all mixed up. How is a conscientious, hard-working secret service agent with a license to kill supposed to know the cowboys from the Indians?

Bond longs for some clear norms, some fixed north for the needle of his moral compass, but finds none. God and the devil used to be helpful images of the two extremes, of good and evil, but these norms he considers manufactured, faded for him. By the end of the book, however, Bond's ethical sophistries have been exploded in his face. The Russian agents have revealed themselves clearly as the villains—villainously evil because they are enemies of England. Now the moral norm is clear. Like a knight on his charger he sets out to defend Britannia, his lady fair. "For love of country" is his creed. All for England are good; all against England are bad.

And so it is throughout the Bond escapades, whether he be fighting Hugo Drax's obliteration-of-London project, Blofield's threat to English

81

livestock and agriculture, or the dastardly plot
to demoralize England with a flood of narcotics.
At times England's inferior allies, America and
France, are involved in the holy crusade against
conspirators from the East. At one point in
the Bond saga, "M" calls upon James to execute
his own private revenge upon ex-Nazis who
have murdered an English couple, friends of
"M." This is clearly not a state affair. But the
job is justified by an appeal to save "face,"
English "face." "If foreign gangsters find they
can get away with this kind of thing they'll
decide the English are as soft as some other
people seem to think we are. . . . These people
can't be hung, sir. But they ought to be killed." [2]

On the Bond beat, the final norm for judging
good or evil is the nation. Fleming's novels
may reflect the sentiments of modern man more
than we realize. The one remaining "ism" for
which many are willing to fight and die is
nationalism. The tendency to put the nation
above everything else so that it becomes the

[2] *For Your Eyes Only*, p. 41.

moral north star in our world of values influences the judgments of the French, the Russians, the English, and the Chinese. Even those who may not be classed as supernationalists are unconsciously influenced by this powerful loyalty of patriotism.

There are real dangers for any country in a narrow nationalism these days. A myopic love of country can stifle healthy criticism and free discussion, the necessary ingredients for a free society. In 1963, Notre Dame University recognized Adlai Stevenson as the American patriot of the year. In the address he gave on that occasion he said,

Our patriotism, our love of country, has to be a discrimination, not a blind force. All too often, voices are raised in the name of some superpatriotism, to still all criticism and to denounce honest divergencies as the next thing to treason. We have risen up from the pit of McCarthy's time, when honest men could lose their jobs for questioning whether there were 381 known Communists in the State Department. But the intolerant spirit which equates responsible criticisms with "selling the country short"

83

or "being soft on communism" or "undermining the American way of life" is still abroad. [8]

Secretary of Defense Robert McNamara, who has been the target of much free-swinging criticism in his conduct of the Viet Nam war, welcomed the criticism as a vital factor in American life. Speaking at his daughter's recent commencement exercise, he pointed out, while pickets marched outside, how desirable it would be if college youth were allowed to picket in Peking and Moscow against the policies of their respective governments. Democracy is predicated on some political consensus fully arrived at in an open public forum of debate and criticism. Those who would stifle such honest difference of opinion in the name of national allegiance and security are really closer to the closed society of Peking and Moscow than the supposed Americanism they espouse.

Frequently the America to be preserved by the narrow nationalists and superpatriots is that part of American life close to their own

[8] "The Hard Kind of Patriotism," *Harpers,* July, 1963, p. 32.

vested self-interest. Much of the antisocialism-
on-the-way-to-Communism complaint linked
with America-firstism is no more than "pocketbook" protection on the part of the wealthy.
"Our instinct is to preserve what we have,
and then to give the instinct a colored wrapping
of patriotism. This is in part what the great
Dr. [Samuel] Johnson meant when he said:
'Patriotism is the last refuge of a scoundrel.' To
defend every abuse, every self-interest, every
encrusted position of privilege in the name of
love of country—when in fact it is only love of
the status quo—that indeed is the lie in the
soul to which any conservative society is
prone." [4]

When the Daughters of the American Revolution prevent Marian Anderson from singing in
Constitution Hall and an American boy of
Mexican descent from carrying the flag in the
color guard, we find it hard to take them
seriously as the great patriots they claim to be.
When leaders of the John Birch Society insinuate
the disloyalty of our presidents, defame the

[4] *Ibid.*, pp. 32-33.

churches, and ridicule the United Nations, we wonder just what kind of America they are trying to preserve. Nationalism may assert itself within the church and compromise its devotion to God. A letter from an Ohio clergyman seems to point in this direction:

An American legionnaire absolutely refuses to come to church now that we have voted that in the sanctuary our flags will be placed so that the position of honor is occupied by the Christian flag instead of the American flag. . . . Along the same line, let me tell you about our early service on the third of July. It is customary for the congregation to remain seated during the singing of the second hymn. Well, I just about had a rebellion on my hands because I did not ask the people to stand up this time. The hymn was "America the Beautiful." It's perfectly all right, apparently, to sit down for "O God, Our Help in Ages Past" but irreverent to do so when we sing about our nation. Incidentally, I have noticed for a number of years that congregations sing patriotic hymns with more spirit than almost any other hymns. Even men and women who usually don't sing at all join in. Is this because these songs are so much better known than any others? I don't think so. It is because our nation is a very real object of love and devotion while God seems vague and unreal. When we sing, a patriotic feeling surges through us that we belong to something great and powerful, but when we sing about God or Christ or the Church we aren't so sure.[5]

All this suggests that the real idol at the center of a paranoid patriotism is the god almighty "I." Our country gives us the opportunity to feel important about ourselves. "Look at me. I am an American or a Frenchman or a Russian." "My country—right or wrong" may mean no more than my point of view, my pocketbook, my vested interests—right or wrong. When we allow the nation to become the final norm for determining between the heroes and the villains, the good guys and the bad guys, as it is with James Bond, then the nation becomes an idol— perhaps no more than a projection of our own idolatrous self-centeredness. "I never was a good son or a good brother or a good patriot," said George Bernard Shaw, "in the sense of thinking that my mother and my sister and my native

[5] Cornelius Loew, *Modern Rivals to Christian Faith* (Philadelphia: The Westminster Press, 1956), pp. 43-44.

country were better than other people's, because I happened to belong to them."

Now what does the Christian ethic have to say about the nation as our ultimate moral norm, as the source of life's meaning, as an end in itself and a law unto itself? Certainly the Bible places the nation, whether it be Israel or Judah, Assyria or Rome, under the sovereign judgment of the Lord of all history. Even Israel, the nation chosen for a special mission, is not excused from God's judgment and punishment. When Israel stepped out of line, the prophets believed that God used the pagan brutality of the Assyrians to punish it. This sounds strangely relevant to our own times, doesn't it?

Some will quote the New Testament words of Jesus, "Render to Caesar the things that are Caesar's, and to God the things that are God's" (Luke 20:25), as if this provides scriptural, divine sanction for God and the state on equal terms. But anyone with any wider understanding of the biblical faith and of the continual conflict between the Christian church and the totalitarian state will set this statement of Jesus in a fuller context. Jesus calls us to "seek first his kingdom and his righteousness, and all these things [including the love of country] shall be yours as well" (Matthew 6:33). The time will come in many different national settings when the Christian will be called upon to obey God rather than men, including the state.

"One nation under God" is not only biblical; it is also true to our best American heritage. Jefferson said, "Indeed, I tremble for my country when I reflect that God is just." And Benjamin Franklin: "Justice is as strictly due between neighbor nations as between neighbor citizens. A highwayman is as much a robber when he plunders in a gang as when single; and a nation that makes an unjust war is only a *great gang*." Let the British who read these pages in criticism of their contemporary hero, James Bond, reflect upon the words of one of their greatest orator-statesmen, Edmund Burke. Looking at the French Revolution from across the channel, he said, "To make us love our country, our country ought to be lovely." According to the Christian political tradition of the West nourished in the

89

biblical faith, there is a norm of good and a source of justice above the state. Every nation stands under the judgment of God. Every nation must seek to obey him. When God is killed by neglect or intention (Nietzsche and Marx) he may be replaced by a totalitarian state like Nazi Germany with its superman myth, or Communist Russia with its myth of historical determinism. "This nation under God" is the biblical and contemporary bastion for democracy, for a free society.

In contrast to a narrow, idolatrous nationalism, there is a true love of country "under God." There is an inevitable attachment to one's homeland—its field of waving grain, its purple mountain majesties, its opportunities for getting ahead, and its continued concern for those who have gotten behind, its malted milks and hamburgers, or perhaps fish and chips.

This is as it should be as long as we keep the proper perspective—"one nation, under God." To love our country under God is to keep her critically aware and steadfastly committed to her dream, her destiny given by God for all mankind. The founders of our American republic believed they were doing something within these shores which raised a hope and promise for the rest of mankind. Lincoln believed God was using the Civil War as a means of protecting that promise, that a government "of the people, by the people, and for the people should not perish from the earth." Stevenson struck the same note: "The patriots are those who love America enough to wish to see her as a model to mankind. This is not treachery. This—as every parent, every teacher, every friend must know—is the truest and noblest affection." If we are to serve God's purpose for our nation we must guard against that simple, inward-looking nationalism which would not allow her to contribute her greatness to the world—the freedom and dignity of man, the rights and responsibilities of a government by the consent of the governed.

A Floridian said to me recently, "I don't like this one-worldism implicit in the United Nations and the ecumenical movement of the churches."

But can there be any other direction for the Christian and also the American? In terms of a democracy for export, a science to be shared, an international trade as necessary for our own economic health, and interdependent defense against Communism, the very self-interest of our nation points toward worldwide cooperation and relationship. Arnold Toynbee insists, "Unless we develop a loyalty to the human race as a whole, we shan't survive." Surely within the nation we have progressed past the utility of a loosely knit confederacy of states, each one a law unto itself, with no strong central government. Now beyond the nation, does not our American hope for all mankind plus our Christian vision of God's Kingdom move us toward a new internationalism? Christian compassion, the concern for peace and justice on earth, knows no national boundaries. God's just and loving purpose overarches the whole family of man. "He made from one every nation of men to live on all the face of the earth . . ." (Acts 17:26). The English nurse Edith Cavell was convicted by the Germans of having assisted British,

French, and Belgian soldiers to escape to England during the First World War. On the night before her execution she expressed the conviction of every Christian for himself and his nation under God: "Patriotism is not enough. I must have no hatred or bitterness towards anyone." U Thant, Secretary General of the United Nations, has said: "The parochial concept of 'our town,' 'our country,' is disappearing. I've been trained to be as objective as possible. If a Burmese boxer, maybe a middleweight, fights a U.S. boxer, I will not feel any emotion. I've reached this stage. It has taken much training and meditation. This should be our aspiration. I feel very strongly about it. If we can think of one human species, it is only wisdom and vision."

To be sure there are dangers of idolatry implicit in the concept and realization of one world as in every structure and system fabricated by man. The best guard against a totalitarian internationalism or a one-world tyranny is the same as the guard against this danger in the nation state: one world *under God*. The God and Father of our Lord Jesus Christ is the source and norm for good over individuals, nations, one world—even the whole universe.

This is surely the Christian vision. God has "made from one every nation of men to live on all the face of the earth." God the Father calls all nations of men to live as sons and brothers, to realize the family spirit. This is why Christians have always contributed to the possibility of international community as expressed in the Holy Roman Empire, the League of Nations, and now the United Nations. It is, again, the vision of Edward Hicks's "Peaceable Kingdom," of Augustine's "City of God," of the Revelation to John: "A great multitude . . . from every nation, from all tribes and peoples and tongues, standing before the throne and before the Lamb . . ." (7:9). For love of country, for all that our nation has to contribute to a wider world community, and for love of God whose purposes for world order far outstrip our narrow nationalisms, we turn from the idolatrous patriotism of James Bond. Under

94

God the nation state cannot be the final norm for good, the major clue as to the heroes and the villains. Neither can some possible future world state be the final arbiter of man's moral values. The God and Father of our Lord Jesus Christ is the ultimate determiner. He calls us to a universal brotherhood which may express itself as a new internationalism or perhaps a world government. The nation state is only a transitional stage of political community on the way to a world community under God.

Again we turn to our former United States ambassador to the United Nations and one of America's most eloquent statesmen after Lincoln. Adlai Stevenson closed his Notre Dame address on "the hard kind of patriotism" with these words:

I can, therefore, wish no more for the profound patriotism of Americans than that they add to it a new dedication to the world-wide brotherhood of which they are a part and that, together with their love of America, there will grow a wider love which seeks to transform our earthly city, with all its races and peoples, all its creeds and aspirations, into Saint Augustine's "Heavenly city where truth reigns, love is the law, and whose extent is eternity."

Thy Kingdom come: thy reign be realized: on earth as it is in heaven. Amen.